THE SHOW

Scott Witmer

Published by ABDO Publishing Company, 8000 West 78th Street, Suite 310, Edina, MN 55439. Copyright ©2010 by Abdo Consulting Group, Inc. International copyrights reserved in all countries. No part of this book may be reproduced in any form without written permission from the publisher. ABDO & Daughters™ is a trademark and logo of ABDO Publishing Company.

Printed in the United States.

PRINTED ON RECYCLED PAPER

Editor: John Hamilton
Graphic Design: Sue Hamilton
Cover Design: John Hamilton
Cover Photo: Getty Images
Interior Photos and Illustrations: Alamy-pg 17; AP-pgs 6, 8, 9, & 12; Corbis-pg 13; Getty Images-pgs 5, 7, 11, 14, 15, 18, 19, 20, 21, 22, 24, 25, 26, 27, 28, & 29; iStockphoto-pg 1; John Hamilton-pg 23; and Jupiterimages-pgs 3, 4, 10, & 16.

Library of Congress Cataloging-in-Publication Data

Witmer, Scott.
  The show / Scott Witmer.
     p. cm. -- (Rock band)
  Includes index.
  ISBN 978-1-60453-695-9
  1. Rock music--Vocational guidance--Juvenile literature. I. Title.
ML3795.W53 2009
781.66'078--dc22
                    0 45.7
                    2009006612

CONTENTS

PREPARATION

Behind the backstage curtains, the band can hear the chanting of the crowd. The time has come to start the show. Together, the band members confidently stride onto the stage, and the crowd's chant becomes a roar. The musicians take their places on stage, adjust their instruments, and begin to play.

What got them here? How did they prepare the stage before the show? What did these musicians do to ready themselves to play their music in front of this crowd? Between scheduling the performance, to the dimming of the lights after the show, what goes into preparing and performing a rock show?

When a rock concert is scheduled, or "booked," a band is usually given an amount of time in which to perform their songs. This collection of songs is called a "set." Sets can vary in length from about 15 minutes to several hours. Normally, musicians playing original music have sets that last about an hour. Cover bands, or bands playing music written by other people, can play several two-hour sets in a night.

> What goes on backstage, before band members take their places on stage?

A lot of work occurs before a band actually takes the stage.

When a band knows how much time they have to play, they create a "set list." This is an ordered list of the songs they'll play at the gig. The arrangement of the set list is very important. Most bands feel that they should open a performance with one of their strongest or most popular songs. This generates excitement in the crowd. And at the end of the set, the band should close with another of their best compositions. When the concert ends, the last song played is usually the most memorable for the audience.

In addition, a set list should include any possible encore songs. An encore is played when the audience cheers loudly and demands more music from the band. Most rock bands save a few of their memorable songs for an encore. For larger touring bands, encores are usually expected. They are less popular with local or newly established bands. Opening acts, or bands that perform before the main act, almost never do an encore.

A set list by American singer-songwriter Bob Dylan. He began the gig with his popular song, "Tangled Up In Blue," and then finished the show with one of his classic and most popular songs, "Blowin' in The Wind."

Bob Dylan performing on stage. As many bands do, he often opens and closes his shows with his most popular tunes.

REHEARSAL

After the set list is complete, the band must rehearse in order to memorize the order of the songs. It's important for each member of the band to be playing the same song! Many bands, especially new groups, will write the set list on a piece of paper and have it with them on stage. Larger touring bands normally play the same show each night, and have memorized the order of the songs.

Rehearsing the set list also establishes how much time the songs will take to play, in order to meet the requirements of the gig. It is important to minimize the time taken between songs. A long time between songs can make the audience lose interest.

Rehearsal is usually conducted as a "dry run" of the performance. If there are any additional theatrics, coordinated movements, or tricks to be performed with the music, they are best perfected before going out on a stage in front of an audience.

> Will.i.am, Fergie, and the rest of the Black Eyed Peas band members rehearsing for a performance at the 2005 Grammy Awards. Rehearsals give bands a chance to coordinate their music with their movements and any special effects.

> The Black Eyed Peas performing at the 2005 Grammy Awards. Everything is carefully rehearsed so the show runs smoothly.

STAGE FRIGHT

Studies have shown that stage fright, or performance anxiety, is the most common phobia in America today. It is very common for musicians to be able to perform flawlessly in rehearsal, but then become very nervous before the actual performance. Sweaty hands, increased nervousness, shortness of breath, and a sense of paralyzing fear are all common symptoms of stage fright.

Psychologists believe that performance anxiety is an instinctual reaction to an upcoming performance. This reaction dates back to prehistoric times, when the body experienced "fight or flight" reactions to predators. In this case, the predator is not a grizzly bear or saber-toothed tiger, but an audience in front of the stage. Blood pressure rises, breathing quickens, and the body's muscles tense and prepare for a confrontation. Understanding this reaction is the best way to fight stage fright.

NUMBER ONE FEAR: PUBLIC SPEAKING

"According to most studies, people's number one fear is public speaking. Number two is death… Does that sound right? This means to the average person, if you go to a funeral, you're better off in the casket than doing the eulogy."
—Jerry Seinfeld

The first thing a performer should do when feeling stage fright coming on is take several deep breaths. This increases oxygen flow to the brain, and slows the heart rate. A very successful method of calming down is to focus on the music, not the audience. Focus on the reason you are there—to perform your music. If you've rehearsed and know your part in the band, then focus on your individual part.

When feeling stage fright, take several deep breaths and focus on the music, not the audience.

Remember that the audience is there to hear your music as a band, not to focus on any mistakes you may make. You are probably your own worst critic. The audience probably will not even notice any small mistakes you might make.

Some musicians drink small sips from a water bottle when they get nervous. This lets them focus on the water bottle and gives them something to do with their hands, instead of wringing them together and being freaked out.

If performance anxiety continues when you reach the stage, keep in mind that it normally lasts only a few minutes into a performance. Once your band hits the stage and starts playing music that you have thoroughly rehearsed, the nervousness tends to calm down.

OUTFITS AND COSTUMES

Rock concerts are not just places to hear music—they are performances. Whether it is for plays, movies, or sports, people enjoy dressing up and performing for others, and audiences enjoy it, too. Rock music is no different. Many rock bands dress up and play a part when they take the stage.

The term "costume" does not necessarily mean anything flamboyant or strange. The Swedish rock group The Hives became known for wearing matching suits on stage. Many of the early rockers of the 1950s and 1960s also wore suits on stage. Country western artists typically wear the standard "country uniform" of cowboy hat, jeans, and cowboy boots.

There are some notable rock acts that took stage costumes to new levels. The band KISS became very famous for their use of makeup and extravagant costumes. The costumes matched their on-stage personas: bassist Gene Simmons was "The Demon," guitarist Paul Stanley was "The Starchild," guitarist Ace Frehley was "The Spaceman," and drummer Peter Criss was "The Catman."

The Swedish rock group The Hives became known for wearing matching suits on stage.

KISS band members became famous for their extravagant makeup and costumes.

In recent years, bands like Slipknot, from Iowa, have put on masks and taken on wild stage personas. But in contrast to the wild costumes worn by some bands, other bands wear their regular street clothes during performances.

The opinions about stage costumes vary greatly in the music industry. Some supporters of wild costumes believe they add to the performance and escapist nature of rock and roll music. Others argue that rock and roll is about the music itself, and not about the clothes worn on stage.

Costumes can seem like a silly gimmick, like the heavy metal band GWAR, or could propel your band into superstardom, like KISS. Regardless of the outfit worn on stage, the presentation should fit the type of music being played. It wouldn't make sense for a singer/songwriter playing an acoustic guitar to wear a leather jumpsuit and a devil clown mask. Likewise, it would seem out of place to watch a hard core metal band playing their songs dressed in collared polo shirts and dress pants. The choice of costume or wardrobe for a performance is ultimately a decision that should be agreed upon by the entire band.

Heavy metal band GWAR became known for their science fiction and horror film style costumes.

Slipknot band members wear masks and take on wild stage personas, much to the delight of their fans.

PROMOTING YOUR BAND

During a concert, there are several things that bands can do to further their music careers (other than playing great music, of course). Large superstar touring acts have professional merchandise vendors that sell T-shirts and band-labeled merchandise. Newer bands usually have to handle this task by themselves. The best time to sell your band's merchandise is before and after a great performance.

T-shirts and CDs are the standard promotional materials sold by newer bands. T-shirts make a great souvenir. People who wear your concert T-shirts promote your band like walking billboards. Usually, there are local printing shops that will offer reasonable rates on printing custom T-shirts. If you can't find a local printer, check out the variety of printing companies that offer their services on the Internet.

The best time to sell your music is right after your band has performed live. If you've put on a good show, the audience should be excited and interested enough to spend money to take your music home with them.

Bands should always have CDs available to purchase at their shows.

> Large touring acts have professional merchandise vendors that sell T-shirts and band-labeled merchandise before, after, and during concerts. Newer bands can handle this task by themselves before and after their time on stage, or with the help of friends.

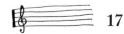

In addition to T-shirts and CDs, there are other promotional products rock bands can offer. Pins and bumper stickers with the band's logo on them have remained popular through the years. Recently, bands have been selling USB flash drives with their music and promotional materials pre-loaded onto them. This is an excellent example of how music promotion has changed with technology.

During the show is also an excellent time to network with other bands. It's common practice for opening bands to thank the headliners while on stage, and vice versa. Showing appreciation and respect to the other bands you're playing with goes a long way to furthering the chances that you'll play together again.

Band members autographing T-shirts for fans. It's important for new bands to have at least CDs and T-shirts available for purchase. This helps keep a band's name remembered and visible.

> Bands may produce many different promotional products, or simply make their CDs available for purchase.

DURING THE SHOW

When rock bands reach superstardom, they have stagehands and roadies who set up the stage for them. The roadies load and unload instruments and equipment. They place the musical gear on the stage, tune the guitars, and change the drumheads. They set up the microphones and microphone stands. They also set up any additional lights and special effects.

The stagehands, or stage managers, then go through and test each instrument and microphone. They make sure that everything is calibrated properly with the venue's sound system. Called a "sound check," this ensures that the audience gets the highest quality music possible from the stage. Unfortunately, newer bands don't have the luxury of seasoned professionals to set up equipment for them.

Roadies setting up a concert stage.

Kyle Falconer, lead singer of The View, is helped out by a roadie. Roadies load and unload instruments and musical gear, as well as set up the stage.

The stage can be a very intimidating place for beginners. When playing a smaller venue, bands are normally required to load and unload their own gear. When a band has loaded all of their equipment on stage and set it up, usually a sound technician will set up microphones for the venue's PA system. The sound tech will place microphones by each guitar amplifier, and several microphones on the drums, in addition to the microphones at the front of the stage used for vocals. Then, the sound tech will start a sound check. Usually, this process involves calling out for each band member to play their instrument separately, and for the drummer to play individual drums. The sound tech will also test the vocal microphones by asking the band members to speak or sing into them.

It is very important to pay attention and be respectful during the sound check. The sound technician is trying to make the band sound good, and a band that goofs around or plays their instruments out of turn during the sound check will probably not sound very good during the performance. Remember, the sound tech is there to help you. Sound checks are also a great time for guitarists to make sure their instruments are in tune.

The Kings of Leon performing a sound check.

On stage, there are several speakers that are turned away from the audience, towards the band. These speakers are called "stage monitors." They are there to help band members hear each other during a performance. For example, the stage monitor near the drummer will help him hear the lead singer and the guitarist. Since the lead singer has his back to the drummer, and the guitarist's amplifier is pointed towards the audience, without the monitor the drummer wouldn't be able to hear them. Monitors are very important in keeping band members in sync with each other, especially during loud performances.

A bass guitar player at an amateur talent show uses two JBL stage monitors to hear the performance.

Stage Monitors

Don't hesitate to tell the sound technician if your monitor needs to be louder or softer. It is okay if your band needs to talk to the sound tech briefly during the performance to adjust your monitor sound, as long as you are respectful about it.

AFTER THE GIG

When your band's set is complete, it's time to remove your equipment, or "break down" the stage. Big-name bands have roadies who do this. The roadies remove all the drums, amplifiers, and instruments, store them carefully in custom crates, and load them into big trucks to be transported to the next gig. Small, newer bands do not have this type of help.

After a set in a music venue, newer bands must remove their own equipment. It is best to do this quickly and orderly. Normally, music venues will feature several bands. If you are not the last band of the night, it is best to be courteous to the other bands and get your stuff off the stage as quickly as possible. The next band can't start setting up until you are completely off the stage.

It is also courteous to make sure you don't leave any trash on stage, including cups, set lists, or discarded drum sticks or guitar strings. This sounds like common sense, but you'd be surprised how many bands don't extend other bands the common courtesy of a quick, clean breakdown. The band that takes the stage after you will remember your courtesy, and will be more likely to invite you to play with them again. Rude bands almost never get invited back to venues or to play with other bands, regardless of how good their music is.

> The "break down" involves packing and removing equipment quickly and orderly, as well as cleaning up the stage.

After removing and storing your band's instruments, it is a great idea to go back into the venue and talk to the crowd. Even superstars have "meet-and-greet" sessions after their concerts. People want to interact with the musicians they have just watched on stage. Meeting with the audience after a show is important to building a relationship with potential fans. People tend to be more excited about musicians whom they feel they know personally. Getting feedback from audience members is also very valuable for the band. Having someone compliment your performance is a fantastic feeling. After the show is the best time to get people's opinions about your music. It's also a great time to sell those T-shirts and CDs!

Meeting the audience after a show is important to building a relationship with potential fans. People tend to be more excited about musicians whom they feel they know personally.

When rock bands first start out, their stage equipment usually consists of little more than instruments and microphones. As bands become larger, so do the stage setups. Additional components are added to the stage show to enhance the performance and experience for the audience. Larger stages can incorporate elaborate stage props and theatrics.

For example, many bands feature large video screens behind the performers, projecting images during the performance. The images can be video of the band performing, video clips that enhance the music, or psychedelic images that give the concert a heightened visual experience. These screens can be huge, like U2's backdrop for their Popmart Tour. The screen was more than 150 feet (46 m) wide and 50 feet (15 m) tall.

The band Bon Jovi performing onstage during Live Earth New York at Giants Stadium. Huge video screens bring the performers up close and personal to everyone attending the concert.

Bono of U2 is dwarfed by his stage set's huge, orange PA speakers.

Bands can also incorporate more elaborate lighting rigs during big concerts. Pink Floyd was famous for their laser lighting shows. Pyrotechnics are also sometimes used. Pyrotechnics are basically large fireworks that are set off either on

The rock band Pink Floyd was famous for their light shows.

or around the stage. The fire and smoke effects can be used to shoot walls of flame or sparks up and around the band during a performance.

In recent years, there have been several accidents with stage pyrotechnics, and their use has become limited. Michael Jackson was injured by pyrotechnics when his hair caught fire in 1984. In 2003, the rock band Great White used spark effects during a show at a club in Rhode Island. The venue caught fire, and 100 people were killed, including the band's guitarist.

Other elaborate stage props include huge characters or sets that interact with the audience. Heavy metal band Iron Maiden is famous for having a huge, zombie-like mascot on stage that moves and sprays smoke or fire. The Rolling Stones featured a huge, inflatable cowgirl that rose up on stage during the song "Honky Tonk Women." Mötley Crüe's drummer, Tommy Lee, had a special drum cage constructed that actually hoisted him and the drums, upside down, over the audience as he played a solo. Several bands have used wire rigs to raise members of the band up into the air over the stage. There is almost no limit to how stage props can be used with the right amount of imagination, innovation, and money.

Elaborate pyrotechnics are often used in rock band shows. However, after a number of deadly accidents in the past, safety has become an all-important concern.

GLOSSARY

ACOUSTIC

When an instrument is played without electronic amplification to make the sound louder. The sound made by the vibrating strings of an acoustic guitar are made louder by resonating inside the hollow body of the instrument.

COVER BAND

A band that plays music that was originally made popular by another band.

GIG

A job as a musician, often a live performance.

GRAMMY AWARD

Yearly awards given out by the National Academy of Recording Arts and Sciences to outstanding artists in various musical categories. The award is named after the gramophone, an early record player.

MEET-AND-GREET SESSION

A time after a concert when band members can meet their fans and get valuable feedback about the performance.

NETWORK

To interact (talk, email, etc.) with other people, especially in order to help your career by exchanging information and contacts. Concerts are a good time to network with other musicians. You never know when somebody might be able to help you. Be nice, and don't be shy!

PHOBIA

An irrational, overwhelming fear of something, like spiders. Stage fright is the fear of performing in front of a crowd. It is a common phobia of musicians.

PROMOTION

An advertising tool that publicizes a band. This makes the public aware of the band's existence, the kind of music it plays, and upcoming concerts.

PYROTECHNICS

Fireworks that are set off during a stage show. Tragedies involving pyrotechnics in recent years have made their use limited today.

ROADIE

A person hired by touring musicians to set up equipment, make sure everything is working properly, and help pack things away after the concert.

SET LIST

A list of songs that a band is scheduled to play at a concert, or gig. The order of the songs is important. Usually, bands open with a popular song to get the crowd excited. The last song played is often from a new album. The set list should also include a possible encore song.

SOUND CHECK

The testing of each instrument and microphone before a concert to make sure the venue's sound system is working properly.

VENUE

The place where a concert is performed.

INDEX